Introduction to Church Membership

Introduction to

CHURCH
Membership

CHURCH OF THE NAZARENE

Nazarene Publishing House
Kansas City, Missouri

Copyright 1999
by Nazarene Publishing House

ISBN 083-411-853X

Printed in the
United States of America

Cover Design: Mike Walsh

10   9   8   7   6   5   4   3   2   1

CONTENTS

Introduction to Church Membership

Welcome to the Church of the Nazarene

We are pleased that you are interested in learning more about the Church of the Nazarene. While there are many communities of faith, we believe our church offers you many positive benefits that will enrich your personal spiritual journey. In this booklet, you will learn more about what we believe, how we practice our faith, and the biblical foundations on which our church is built.

Essential to fellowship in any Nazarene church is a vital relationship with Jesus Christ. If you have not already received Christ into your life as your Savior, the steps to take are clearly stated in the Bible.

First, recognize and admit your need of Jesus. The Bible says, *For all have sinned and fall short of the glory of God, and are justified freely by his grace through the redemption that came by Christ Jesus* (Rom. 3:23-24). According to the Bible, every person is a sinner by birth as well as by choice. God's law condemns us because both our actions as well as our motives are imperfect before Him. But there is more!

Our sin carries an awesome penalty. The Bible says, *For the wages of sin is death* (Rom. 6:23). Faced with this, the news for humankind is not good. Since everyone has sinned and fallen short of God's glory, we all face the same penalty, death. The death penalty that accompanies sin is more than just the end of our physical existence. It includes eternal separation from God. Imagine living in an environment where one was cut off from all that is good and wholesome! But there is good news!

Second, accept Christ's love and forgiveness that He extends to you. The Bible puts it this way: *You see, at just the right time, when we were still powerless, Christ died for the ungodly. Very rarely will anyone die for a righteous man, though for a good man someone might possibly dare to die. But God demonstrates his own love for us in this: While we were still sinners, Christ died for us* (Rom. 5:6-8, emphasis added).

God cannot overlook sin. Sin is much more than personal or social dysfunction. The Bible tells us that sin devastates and destroys everything it touches. It will ruin personal, family, and social life, for *the heart is deceitful above all things and beyond cure. Who can understand it?* (Jer. 17:9). Countless numbers of individuals, families, and societies have experienced the effects of sin, from simple disruption to the disasters of genocide!

The good news is that God in His mercy and grace sent Jesus Christ, His Son, to experience the full effect of sin by dying on the Cross for us. Jesus experienced death and separation from God the Father in order that we might be saved. He gave His life as a sacrifice for us, and through His death, we can be forgiven and restored to fellowship with God.

We must accept Christ by trusting Him, confessing our sins, and repenting of them. The Bible says, *God's kindness leads you toward repentance* (Rom. 2:4). The *Manual of the Church of the Nazarene* states: *We believe that repentance, which is a sincere and thorough change of the mind in regard to sin, involving a sense of personal guilt and a voluntary turning away from sin, is demanded of all who have by act or purpose become sinners against God. The Spirit of God gives to all who will repent the gracious help of penitence of heart and hope of mercy, that they may believe unto pardon and spiritual life* (29-30).

The final step in conversion is to believe. Faith in Jesus Christ is the key to conversion. It is more, however, than just intellectual assent regarding some popular belief about the person of Jesus Christ. Merely believing that Jesus is God is insufficient faith. The Bible states: *You believe that there is one God. Good! Even the demons believe that—and shudder* (James 2:19). Believing in Jesus, trusting Jesus to be your Savior, the One who forgives sins, requires a deep commitment from one's inner being. That's why Nazarenes believe in repentance. Repentance, which means a thorough change of mind and heart, including the direction of one's life, combines with personal faith and trust in Jesus to bring us salvation.

The Bible puts it this way: *If you confess with your mouth, "Jesus is Lord," and believe in your heart that God raised him from the dead, you will be saved. For it is with your heart that you believe and are justified, and it is with your mouth that you confess and are saved. As the Scripture says, "Anyone who trusts in him will never be put to shame." . . . For, "Everyone who calls on the name of the Lord will be saved"* (Rom. 10:9-11, 13).

If you have given your heart and life to Jesus, there is one more piece of good news: *Therefore, there is now no condemnation for those who are in Christ Jesus, because through Christ Jesus the law of the Spirit of life set me free from the law of sin and death* (Rom. 8:1-2). As one who has been forgiven by Christ, we have *redemption through his blood, the forgiveness of sins, in accordance with the riches of God's grace that he lavished on us with all wisdom and understanding* (Eph. 1:7-8).

Ready to Meet Some New Friends?

Foundations of Faith

As Christians, we are family. As members of the Church of the Nazarene our faith rests on common ground. Here at the very beginning, let's take a look at the foundations of our faith and how they relate to believers celebrating our common faith in Christ. On these foundations, we worship, serve, and work for the growth of the kingdom of God.

✧ Meeting God through Jesus Christ

While it may appear unnecessary to discuss this point, it must not be taken for granted. Conversion, being born again, trusting Christ as one's personal Savior is crucial to Nazarenes. Every member of the Church of the Nazarene must be clear regarding his or her personal salvation. Eternal salvation is provided to us, free, without cost, simply on the basis of trusting Christ who died on the Cross to save whoever would believe in Him.

> **Scriptures about salvation to look up**
>
> Luke 18:14; John 1:12-13; 3:3-8; 5:24; Rom.
> 1:17; 3:21-26
>
> Discuss: (1) On what basis are we saved?
> (2) What does justification mean?

✧ Trusting Christ for personal salvation

Did you ever wonder where our name came from? In the New Testament Book of Matthew, what little we know about the childhood and boyhood of Jesus includes a story of how His parents moved to Egypt for His protection. They did this in order to avoid the horrible persecution of Herod, who was ruler of Judea, where Jesus and His parents lived. When Herod died, Archelaus, his son, assumed the position of authority held by his father. Joseph was fearful that Archelaus might try to find Jesus and kill Him.

At the appropriate time, in response to divine direction, Joseph moved the family back to Israel. In a dream, he was warned to move to the northern area of Israel in the district of Galilee. Matthew 2:23 reads, *And he went and lived in a town called Nazareth. So was fulfilled what was said through the prophets: "He will be called a Nazarene."*

When our founder, Phineas Bresee, was considering a name, all of the gracious, compassionate characteristics of Jesus were embodied in his dream of what a church should be like. From there it was only a small step to call the new movement God was raising up *The Church of the Nazarene.* And so, today, we are known simply as *Nazarenes.*

There is something wonderful about that name! *The Nazarene,* as Jesus was known, indicated much about who He was. He was not from the religious and cultural capital of Israel, which was Jerusalem. Although He was born in Bethlehem, it was Nazareth in the north that stuck to Him as His primary identifier. Nothing as significant as the Messiah was ever expected to come out of the Galilee district of the nation. Yet this simple carpenter, with His close friends and His uncommon message, changed the world.

For Nazarenes, Jesus Christ is central to our story. He is the Son of God. He is the Savior of the world. His Word endures forever. His ethic informs our values and characterizes our conduct. His resurrection guarantees our future. Someday we will stand before Him in eternity and be judged by Him.

Scriptures concerning Jesus Christ to look up

(1) 2 Cor. 5:17
(2) Gal. 3:1-14
(3) What does it mean to become a new creation?
(4) Discuss the work Jesus did on the Cross for us.

✧ *Believing and obeying God's Word to us*

The Bible is very important to Nazarenes. We believe that it is fully inspired and contains everything we need to know about eternal salvation. It tells us, clearly and simply, how to come to God through Jesus Christ. It tells us how to live as followers of Jesus. To us, the Bible is a living book. We believe it is God's Word. Indeed John, in describing Jesus, wrote, *In the beginning was the Word, and the Word was with God, and the Word was God. He was with God in the beginning. . . . The Word became flesh and made his dwelling among us. We have seen his glory, the glory of the One and Only, who came from the Father, full of grace and truth* (John 1:1-2, 14).

Nazarenes believe that Scripture reveals the eternal, Living Word, who is Jesus Christ. The Scriptures tell us of God's grace, compassion, and purpose. They tell of how God's purpose has reached its fulfillment in the life, death, and resurrection of Jesus. Nazarenes trust the Word of God, just as they trust the Christ who is the Living Word that is revealed to us in the sacred words of the Bible.

Scriptures about the Bible, God's Word

(1) Luke 24:44-47
(2) 1 Pet. 1:10-12

Discuss:

"We believe in the plenary inspiration of the Holy Scriptures, by which we understand the 66 books of the Old and New Testaments, given by divine inspiration, inerrantly revealing

> the will of God concerning us in all things necessary to our salvation, so that whatever is not contained therein is not to be enjoined as an article of faith" (*Manual,* Articles of Faith, IV, 27).

✧ *Sharing truth in personal commitment*

While Nazarenes are members of a spiritual community of like-minded believers called the local church, we emphasize the personal dimension of our faith commitment. Individual faith, belief, and personal piety are important to Nazarenes. The Body of Christ as expressed in the fellowship and mission of the local church is made up of the individual and personal faith commitments of each believer.

There is an old adage that says a chain is no stronger than its weakest link. For this reason, that is, the fact that we are knit together into a living organism, the vitality and health of each member's personal spiritual experience is important.

> **Discuss:**
>
> "To be identified with the visible Church is the blessed privilege and sacred duty of all who are saved from their sins and are seeking completeness in Christ Jesus" (*Manual,* The General Rules, 36).
>
> (1) How can we help each other grow in Christ?

> **(2) How does membership in the local church facilitate the spiritual growth of every member?**

✥ Finding fellowship for our journey

A fellowship must rest upon common values. In other words, all who are members of that fellowship must find a common reference point to which they can point as something they all share.

✥ Responding positively to the upward call

"They call us Holiness people. That's good. That's another thing I love about Nazarenes. Wherever I hear a Nazarene choir sing, hear a Nazarene pastor preach, visit a Nazarene college chapel service, or enjoy the delights of a Nazarene potluck dinner, I know I am with people who take to heart our Savior's call to holiness. I look at their faces and know they have met the Lord in a saving encounter, that they would not willingly do anything wrong. These are people who grieve when they fail, who make the pursuit and possession of sanctifying grace life's chief priority. No casual sinning, no cheap grace, no glib discipleship here—these are Nazarenes" (Wesley D. Tracy and Stan Ingersol, *Here We Stand* [Kansas City: Beacon Hill Press of Kansas City, 1999], 16-17).

Nazarenes believe in a second work of grace. While it is known by a variety of names, *entire sanctification* is one that is cited frequently. Tracy and Ingersol describe it this way:

> **"Entire sanctification represent(s) a real cleansing—a real grace in this life—that conquers sin. Every other Christian doctrine (is) somehow related to this one, and no method (can) be employed that contradict(s) it. The deep awareness of sin, repentance, the regenerating power of the new birth, life in the Spirit, true eucharistic celebration—all (are) related to entire sanctification" (ibid., 24).**

The upward call of our new life in Christ is energized by the presence of the Holy Spirit in our lives. As we respond positively and completely to His leadership, we are drawn upward toward those scriptural values that lay at the core of Nazarene beliefs and practices. Simply put, the founders of the Church of the Nazarene knew that "keeping rules could not save them. *But they [also] recognized that ethical conduct is important when it comes to stewardship, discipleship, and witness"* (ibid., 25, emphasis added).

Scriptures to look up

(1) John 15:1-11
(2) Rom. 12:1—15:3
(3) Eph. 4:17—5:20

> (4) Jer. 31:31-34
>
> (5) Ezek. 36:25-27
>
> **Review:**
>
> (1) When is a person entirely sanctified?
>
> (2) What must a person do to be entirely sanctified?
>
> (3) What can a sanctified believer expect?
>
> (4) What are some resources for living this deeper life?

✧ *Embracing our world with a Christ-centered vision*

> "Wherever I go, I run into family, the great Nazarene family who put their arms around the world and create homelike churches. I love the family atmosphere at least as much as our theology and our 'get things done' attitude. We are a covenant community of faith. Everywhere you drop in on Nazarenes, you get bright-eyed welcomes and hugs as if you were the last person to show up at a family reunion" (ibid., 14).

The Nazarene family has always looked beyond its own doorsteps. It has always believed that *"the world is our parish."*

> "The Church—our church—has just four things to do: worship, evangelism, nurture, and service. Armed and energized by their Christian, Protestant, Wesleyan-Holiness heritage and

theology, Nazarenes everywhere busily carry out their fourfold task" (ibid., 32).

Characterized by lively worship, a deep abiding interest in winning people to Christ, and a commitment to facilitating spiritual growth in believers, Nazarene churches are beacons of light and hope for our world. Beyond this, however, is a persistent concern for others.

"John Wesley declared, 'I do not acknowledge him to have one grain of faith who is not continually . . . willing to spend and be spent in doing all good . . . to all men.' Phineas F. Bresee in 1901 wrote in the *Nazarene Messenger*, 'The evidence of the presence of Jesus in our midst is that we bear the gospel, primarily, to the poor.' Later he added, 'I may have faith that moves mountains, and if I lack the great love that stoops to lift men, I am nothing—*no thing*'" (ibid., 36).

Vital Piety

Membership in the Church of the Nazarene points to the distinct values of vital piety as hallmarks of our fellowship.

"It is required of all who desire to unite with the Church of the Nazarene, and thus to walk in fellowship with us, that they shall show evidence of salvation from their sins by a godly

> walk and vital piety; and that they shall be, or
> earnestly desire to be, cleansed from all in-
> dwelling sin" (*Manual,* The General Rules, 36).

Vital piety as noted in the above statement, taken from the *Manual of the Church of the Nazarene,* is a key word that really describes the foundation on which our fellowship as Nazarenes rests.

> "[John] Wesley was aware that new birth into
> Christ can degenerate into sentimental emo-
> tionalism, ineffective religiosity, or irrelevant
> piety" (Thomas Langford, *Practical Divinity*
> [Nashville: Abingdon Press, 1983], 42).

Vital piety is living piety that is expressed every day in real-world situations. Nazarenes do not believe in hothouse religion.

The common, shared values, on which our fellowship is based, involve both positive and negative expressions. The positive is expressed this way:

> "FIRST. By doing that which is enjoined in the
> Word of God, which is our rule of both faith
> and practice" (*Manual,* The General Rules, 36).

Under the heading of this section of the *Manual,* Nazarenes are urged to:

- Love God with all one's heart
- Share Christ with those who do not know Him
- Be courteous to all people

- Help each other with an attitude of loving-kindness

- Meet needs wherever they are with whatever we have

- Contribute to the financial support of our local church

Clearly, this is a commitment to a living relationship to Christ that is expressed in everyday relationships with friends, church members, and those who do not know Jesus Christ as Savior. A church fellowship based on these values enriches the spiritual experiences of its membership, while simultaneously ministering to the community and world at large.

The second element of our General and Special Rules may be summarized simply as an instruction to be *avoiding evil of every kind* (*Manual*, The General Rules, 37). Wesley Tracy and Stan Ingersol have summed it up this way:

"The Special Rules (*Manual*, pars. 33-41) represent the church's effort to interpret and apply its Articles of Faith and General Rules to specific needs of a changing culture. Currently, the Special Rules speak against all "entertainments that are subversive of the Christian [life]" (34.1), gambling, membership in oath-bound secret organizations, social dancing, using tobacco or intoxicating drinks, divorce, abortion, and sexual perversions such as homosexual activity or pornographic uses of sex in marriage (34.2-37). The Special Rules speak in favor of

Christian marriage, sex as a gift of God, Christian stewardship, storehouse tithing, and support of pastors and other ministers" (*Here We Stand*, 32).

To say we're glad you've decided to investigate the Church of the Nazarene would be an understatement. Sometime ago, we ran an advertising campaign with the catchy slogan, *Welcome to the Church of the Nazarene—Our Church Can Be Your Home!* As a denomination with global congregations, as well as a local church down the street from where you live, we are here for you. We are interested in you both as a person as well as a potential church member.

"You yourself may not know what you need to know about the Christian faith. We have a rich heritage and an adequate theology that speaks with faith and reason and precedent to the social, religious, economic, and spiritual problems that bedevil our times. You need to know that you don't have to figure all these things out from scratch. Your faith has resources, but if you don't know your faith, you're condemned to struggle with reinventing the wheel" (ibid., 13).

The Nazarene Family Tree

In 18th-century England, three Church of England clergymen—John Wesley, his brother Charles, and George Whitefield—were mightily used by God to bring spiritual revival to England. This was a time of great upheaval as England was moving through the social impact of the industrial revolution. Children were often mistreated. Family units broke down under the sheer weight of impossible economic conditions and the unimpeded flow of godless social conditions. Through the ministries of these three, and especially John Wesley, a time of revival and reform began. It overflowed to the newly founded nation of the United States of America.

"From roots in the Wesleyan revival in 18th-century England, the Holiness Movement blossomed in America. Wesleyan-Holiness denominations sprang up in every section of the country. Three such denominations and substantial parts of two other groups joined together in 1907 (Chicago) and 1908 (Pilot Point, Texas) to form the Church of the Nazarene.

"Key leaders were Phineas F. Bresee [first among equals and the personality that energized the union], C. B. Jernigan, C. W. Ruth, and H. F. Reynolds, among others.

"The dream that drew the founders together was a believers' church in the Wesleyan tradition. This was fleshed out with firm beliefs in orthodox Christianity. Traditional doctrines of the inspiration of the Bible; the Holy Trinity; the deity of Christ; and Protestant beliefs in *sola scriptura* (Scripture alone) as the Rule of faith and practice; *sola gratia*, salvation by grace alone; *sola fidei*, faith alone; and the priesthood of all believers marked the new Nazarene denomination.

"The Wesleyan doctrine of salvation, particularly entire sanctification, became the foundation for theology, worship, evangelism, nurture, service, and church administration" (ibid., 20).

Phineas F. Bresee and Other Early Leaders

In October 1895, Phineas F. Bresee and Joseph P. Widney, M.D., organized the Church of the Nazarene at Los Angeles. With approximately 100 members, Bresee did not believe he was merely beginning an independent church. Indeed he *saw this church as the first of a denomination that preached the reality of entire sanctification received through faith in Christ* (*Manual*, Historical Statement, 18). Bresee was literally following in the footsteps of John Wesley. Bresee foresaw the development of a denomination and worked to ensure its continuity and strength in the organizational structure he provided. The Church of the Nazarene spread along the West Coast, eventually scattering across the continent as far east as Illinois.

Merging and Uniting—the Church of the Nazarene Takes Shape

The first of two merging/uniting events took place at the General Assembly in Chicago from October 10 to 17, 1907. This body adopted the name The Pentecostal Church of the Nazarene and elected Hiram F. Reynolds and Phineas F. Bresee as its general superintendents.

The second General Assembly met in a joint session with the General Council of the Holiness Church of Christ from October 8 to 14 in 1908 at Pilot Point, Texas. On the morning of October 13, these two bodies merged and became the Pentecostal Church of the Nazarene. At the General Assembly of 1919, the denomination voted to officially change its name to Church of the Nazarene, *because of new meanings that had become associated with the term "Pentecostal"* (*Manual*, Historical Statement, 20).

Over the years eight additional groups joined the Church of the Nazarene in testimony of God's direction and leadership upon this young, growing denomination. And the growth of the church included others outside North America. England and Scotland, along with Canada, added to the growing number of churches. With seven world regions and eight regions within the U.S.A., the Church of the Nazarene has grown to become a global family.

The official handbook of Church of the Nazarene is the *Manual*. It contains more than just the history of the church. It contains the Constitution, Articles of Faith, Articles of Organization, and the Government of the church.

> "The Church of the Nazarene exists to serve as an instrument for advancing the kingdom of God through the preaching and teaching of the gospel throughout the world. Our well-defined commission is to preserve and propagate Christian holiness as set forth in the Scriptures, through the conversion of sinners, the reclamation of backsliders, and the entire sanctification of believers.
>
> "Our objective is a spiritual one, namely, to evangelize as a response to the Great Commission of our Lord to 'go and make disciples of all nations' (Matthew 28:19; cf. John 20:21; Mark 16:15). We believe that this aim can be realized through agreed-upon policies and procedures, including doctrinal tenets of faith and time-tested standards of morality and lifestyle" (*Manual*, Foreword, 5).

You will want to obtain a copy of the *Manual* for your personal study.

For Review:

(1) Read the Agreed Statement of Belief (*Manual,* The Church, IV, 35-36).

(2) Read the General and Special Rules in the *Manual.*

Nazarenes in Action

When you become a member of the Church of the Nazarene, you become a part of a global family. In order to fulfill the mission of our church, the Nazarene family is organized for action and mission in three ways. In this section we will examine the following:

✦*THE LOCAL CHURCH*
- ❑ Organization
- ❑ Administration
- ❑ Function and Purpose
- ❑ Linkages

✦*THE GLOBAL COMMUNITY OF FAITH*
- ❑ The District
- ❑ The Region
- ❑ The General Assembly

✦*THE RESOURCES FOR FULFILLING OUR GLOBAL MISSION*
- ❑ The Ministry of the People of God (elders, deacons, and laity united in ministry)
- ❑ Agencies for Fulfilling the Mission
- ❑ Communicating the Good News
- ❑ Equipping and Enabling Global Mission
- ❑ Responding to Need

The Local Church

With approximately 11,900 congregations, the Church of the Nazarene reaches out in ministry and service to approximately 1.5 million members in more than 125 countries. Each local church has a church board, composed of stewards and trustees. Stewards typically care for a variety of ministries of the local church, while trustees attend to business matters. While these distinctions are derived from the *Manual of the Church of the Nazarene,* the board functions as a unit in caring for the needs of the congregation. In addition to stewards and trustees, the president of the local Nazarene Youth International Ministries, the Nazarene World Mission Society president, and the Sunday School superintendent are also members of the church board. Each local church elects its own leadership at the annual church meeting. Various other boards, councils, and committees are elected or appointed to provide general oversight of local church ministries and programs. Each local church calls its own pastor by congregational vote and with the approval of the district superintendent.

The District

Each local church is located within the boundaries of a district. The district is comprised of all the churches within its boundary. Local churches elect representatives called delegates to attend the annual district assembly. Each local church supports the collective ministries of the district through an amount of money shared annually for district administration. Each district elects a district superintendent, who cares for the ministry emphasis for that area. A District Advisory Board composed equally of laypersons and ministers considers the various ministry, stewardship, and legal matters pertaining to the district. At the district assembly, delegates vote on various boards and committees, the leadership of the district, and every four years, they elect delegates to the General Assembly.

General Assembly

Every four years, delegates from all the districts of the Church of the Nazarene from every part of the world meet for General Assembly. This event permits members of the Church of the Nazarene to worship together as a global family. This is a time for celebrating our solidarity and brotherhood, while at the same time selecting our global leaders, determining administrative policy, and generally preparing our global mission strategy. Legislative issues pertaining to efficiency in ministry and mission are discussed and adopted; leadership for the denomination is selected as well. Six general superintendents are elected by ballot by the delegates. Along with the general superintendents, a General Board, equally composed of laypersons and ministers, and representing the global regions of ministry, is selected.

Annually, the General Board meets to address various ministry and administrative needs for the

Church of the Nazarene. In addition to this, missionaries to various world areas are recommended and appointed for terms of service. To support the global ministry of the Church of the Nazarene, local congregations participate by giving their financial support to the World Evangelism Fund. The General Board oversees the allocation of funds to insure that ministry interests are primary.

Additional Resources for Mission Fulfillment

Fundamental to fulfilling our global mission are the parallel ministries of both laypersons and clergy. While the Church of the Nazarene recognizes the biblical description of individuals set apart for functional roles of ministry, we also recognize the fact that every believer is a minister. Elders are ordained clergy whose primary ministry centers on the proclamation of God's Word. Deacons are ordained ministers whose primary focus is on service and support ministries. All Christians form what Peter refers to as the *priesthood* of believers (1 Pet. 2:9). Peter describes this priesthood as *living stones . . . being built into a spiritual house to be a holy priesthood, offering spiritual sacrifices acceptable to God through Jesus Christ* (v. 5).

Additionally, the Church of the Nazarene operates a number of agencies designed to further our response to global mission. At the International Headquarters in Kansas City, Missouri, U.S.A., the Sunday School Ministries Division, Communications Division, Evangelism and Church Growth Division, along with the World Mission Division, facilitate the global effort of making disciples of Jesus Christ. Nazarene Publishing House with its subsidiary business units provides a variety of tools in various media to support global evangelism and disciple-making initiatives.

Jesus told His disciples to look and see the fields that were *ripe* and ready *for harvest* (John 4:35). The global harvest fields require a workforce. On each region, there are Nazarene colleges or universities with the stated mission of equipping students for life. While not all graduates attend seminary to become clergy or missionaries, each student is provided the opportunity to learn how life can be lived as a steward of God's grace in a busy world. Over 50 institutions of higher education represent the Church of the Nazarene's commitment to preparing students for excellence in their chosen fields of endeavor.

You know that a candle by itself can succeed in giving enough light for its owner. When candles are lit and brought together, they give light enough to dispel the darkness. A solitary Christian is like the solitary candle. Without the support and mutual edification of others, the light of faith may dim or burn out. Joined together, believers increase their capacity to give light exponentially. And their mutual fellowship enriches their individual profession of faith as well as expanding and energizing their capacity for extensive mission and ministry.

Review the following:

(1) Ask your pastor to show you a copy of the district journal from the district in which your church is located.

(2) Ask your pastor to discuss district assembly and General Assembly.

(3) Review your local church's annual report to learn more about the annual meeting where local church leadership is selected.

Fellowships of Transformation, Compassion, and Kindness

Nazarenes have succeeded in organizational formats that have helped us reach many people for Christ. Perhaps it would be easy to overlook what really drives our passion. It is not simply to organize for the sake of organization. We believe that Jesus Christ wants us to model Him, so that as He was in the world, so we should be in the world as His representatives. Wherever there is need, it is our opportunity to meet that need in Jesus' name. Wherever there are people who have not heard the story of Jesus, it is our responsibility to go and proclaim the Good News in word and action.

Principle-Centered and Mission-Driven

Nazarene churches believe in teaching the Bible across generational lines. Sunday Schools, small groups, Bible study fellowships, all meet with the singular purpose of teaching God's Word. While we believe the world is our parish, we also believe in beginning our mission right at home in our own backyard.

Boys and girls, teens, young people, in fact, people of all ages must hear and learn about Christ.

I have chosen to call this section *Fellowships of Transformation, Compassion, and Kindness.* In reality, Nazarenes believe strongly in these three values. In this section we will look at the manner in which our church is organized, for there you will discover that these values really do lie at the heart of our being as a denomination.

The Church of the Nazarene has a representative form of government. This simply means that each local church, while enjoying certain rights and privileges, exists along with all other Nazarene churches in a linked fellowship of global mission.

> "Each church shall enjoy the right to select its own pastor, subject to such approval as the General Assembly shall find wise to institute. Each church shall also elect delegates to the various assemblies, manage its own finances, and have charge of all other matters pertaining to its local life and work" (*Manual,* Articles of Organization and Government, par. 28.2, 38).

Nazarenes that have reached their 15th birthday are eligible to vote in church elections. We enjoy the double benefits of expressing the life and work of our local church in ways that respond to the needs and opportunities around us. Additionally, we enjoy fellowship and mutual participation in a global fellowship of like-minded believers in Nazarene churches around the world. The representational form of government gives us freedom while preserving the integrity of our beliefs and practices in the context of global mission.

As a fellowship of transformation, we agree to uphold biblically based principles in everyday life and living. Our church is nonsectarian in that (1) we embrace the historic creeds of Christendom, and (2) we see ourselves within the great stream of biblical Christianity.

> "The task of the Church of the Nazarene is to make known to all peoples the transforming grace of God through the forgiveness of sins and heart cleansing in Jesus Christ. Our mission first and foremost is to 'make disciples,' to incorporate believers into fellowship and membership (congregations), and to equip (teach) for ministry all who respond in faith. The ultimate goal of the community of faith is to 'present everyone perfect in Christ' (Colossians 1:28) at the last day.
>
> "It is in the local church that the saving, perfecting, teaching, and commissioning takes place. The local church, the Body of Christ, is the representation of our faith and mission" (*Manual*, Preamble, 56).

It is easy to see how Nazarenes have come to view their local churches as important links in a chain of hope and transformation that now stretches around the world. Our churches are truly "principle-centered and mission-driven." Our task is spelled out clearly in the above-cited Preamble. Making Christ known to all peoples is at the heart of who we are as a people and a denomination.

After evangelism comes discipleship. Christian formation, or the spiritual development of believers as members of the Body of Christ, is an equally important mission and task of the local church. How is this accomplished?

Your involvement in the church can be as extensive or limited as you choose. Serious Christian discipleship requires participation in the various means of grace that are available to help you achieve significant spiritual growth in Christ. Sunday School classes offer opportunities for learning about your faith in the context of a caring fellowship and small group. Here you will discover a Bible-centered curriculum that is geared to bringing about life change in the direction of God's plan and provision. Sunday School classes are geared to the needs of their participants. The levels of readiness, experience, and knowledge of the Bible are just some of the elements taken into consideration by our Sunday School classes and teachers. Sunday School classes provide safe, nonthreatening ways of getting involved in the wider fellowship of the church. By getting acquainted with a small group of friends in a Sunday School class, it becomes easier to move out into the larger fellowship of the church.

Many Nazarene churches offer small-group Bible studies, care groups, and other means for helping each other grow in Christ and be equipped to serve Him effectively. Check the schedule of services for your church. In addition to Sunday School and Bible study fellowship groups, you will discover public worship times along with midweek opportunities for spiritual enrichment.

The Means of Grace

While we trust Christ for personal salvation, our experience is that of being in community with other believers. In other words, our experience is not that of solitary profession of faith, but rather, communal participation in all the means of grace. What are the means of grace?

- Public worship every Sunday is a very special means of grace for all believers. As Nazarenes we cannot neglect our meeting together for public worship and fellowship. Our worship times include praise to God, worship of His majesty and holiness, and encounter with His will for our lives through listening to the proclamation of His Word.

- The Church of the Nazarene observes the sacraments of Holy Communion and baptism. When the Body of Christ receives the sacrament of Communion, we participate in a special observance of holy fellowship instituted by our Lord when He was among us.

"We believe that the Memorial and Communion Supper instituted by our Lord and Savior Jesus Christ is essentially a New Testament sacrament, declarative of His sacrificial death, through the merits of which believers have life and salvation and promise of all spiritual bless-

> ings in Christ" (*Manual*, Articles of Faith, XIII, 33).

Nazarenes believe baptism is also a special means of grace indicating a believer's intention to follow Jesus, and is indicative of personal repentance, confession, and faith in Christ.

> "We believe that Christian baptism, commanded by our Lord, is a sacrament signifying acceptance of the benefits of the atonement of Jesus Christ, to be administered to believers and declarative of their faith in Jesus Christ as their Savior, and full purpose of obedience in holiness and righteousness" (*Manual*, Articles of Faith, XII, 32).

● Nazarenes also believe in Christian stewardship.

> "The Scriptures teach that God is the Owner of all persons and all things. We, therefore, are His stewards of both life and possessions. God's ownership and our stewardship ought to be acknowledged, for we shall be held personally accountable to God for the exercise of our stewardship" (*Manual*, Special Rules, 51).

This is why we practice tithing, giving God 10 percent of our income as an act of worship and stewardship.

> "Storehouse tithing is a scriptural and practical performance of faithfully and regularly placing the tithe into that church to which the member belongs. Therefore, the financing of the church shall be based on the plan of storehouse tithing, and the local Church of the Nazarene shall be regarded by all of its people as the storehouse. All who are a part of the Church of the Nazarene are urged to contribute faithfully one-tenth of all their increase as a minimum financial obligation to the Lord and freewill offerings in addition as God has prospered them for the support of the whole church, local, district, regional, and general" (*Manual*, Special Rules, 52).

- Nazarenes believe in personal, family, and corporate prayer. We urge believers to develop personal devotional times for Bible study and prayer. We encourage family prayer times when the whole family can be together for a time of spiritual worship and fellowship. Corporate prayer represents the public worship times when we come as the Body of Christ in worship, adoration, and obedience to God.

Organized for Mission

In order to represent Christ faithfully in our world, Nazarene churches organize their efforts for increased effectiveness. A local board governs each local church.

"Every local church shall have a church board, composed of the pastor, the Sunday School superintendent, the president of the Nazarene Youth International, the president of the Nazarene World Mission Society . . . , the stewards, and the trustees of the church. . . . The business of the church board shall be: (1) To care for the interests of the church and its work. . . . (2) To nominate . . . the proper person to become pastor. . . . (3) To cooperate with an incoming pastor in the development of a written statement of goals. . . . (4) To conduct at least once every two years . . . a self-study. . . . (5) To arrange for pastoral supply. . . . (6) To provide for the development . . . of an annual budget for the church [and] all auxiliaries [and many other important tasks]" *(Manual,* The Local Church, K, 75-79).

Families, teens, children, senior adults, singles—all make up our world. The needs of all must be addressed in settings and forums that provide adequate responses of the various ministries of the local church. Nazarene churches have youth groups, the Nazarene Youth International; missions groups, the Nazarene World Mission Society; children's groups, Caravans; senior adult groups, Prime Time and Senior Adult Ministries (SAM); these are known as auxiliaries.

Each of the auxiliaries has its own constitution, local organization, district organization, and regional component. Every four years, the NYI, NWMS, and Sunday School meet during the General Assembly for international conventions.

As fellowships of transformation, compassion, and kindness, the Church of the Nazarene embraces and expresses the twin commands of Jesus when He said, *"'Love the Lord your God with all your heart and with all your soul and with all your mind.' This is the first and greatest commandment. And the second is like it: 'Love your neighbor as yourself.' All the Law and the Prophets hang on these two commandments"* (Matt. 22:37-40).

Nazarene churches provide more than just instruction, worship, and discipleship activities. Nazarenes are involved in providing disaster relief, compassionate action wherever it is needed, and mercy ministries to those less fortunate than us. Nazarenes embrace reconciliation, bridge building, and peacemaking efforts.

A Nazarene is one who takes seriously both the Great Commission and the Great Commandment. The final commission Jesus gave to the Church was a directive to share the Good News with the whole world.

"Then Jesus came to them and said, 'All authority in heaven and on earth has been given to me. Therefore go and make disciples of all nations, baptizing them in the name of the Father and of the Son and of the Holy Spirit, and teaching them to obey everything I have commanded you. And surely I am with you always, to the very end of the age'" (Matt. 28:18-20).

Welcome to the Church of the Nazarene. May you discover in our fellowship Christ's transforming power and His compassionate mercy in all that we say and do. May our hearts be knit together in a fellowship of holy love.

"My purpose is that they may be encouraged in heart and united in love, so that they may have the full riches of complete understanding, in order that they may know the mystery of God, namely, Christ, in whom are hidden all the treasures of wisdom and knowledge" (Col. 2:2-3).

Review:

1. What does representational form of government mean?
2. What does nonsectarian mean?
3. Reread the Preamble in the *Manual,* and state the central task of the Church of the Nazarene in your own words.
4. Invite your Sunday School superintendent to talk about Sunday School classes in your church.
5. Meet with your church's NYI and NWMS presidents. Ask them to tell you about their respective ministries.
6. Discuss the means of grace available to Nazarenes.
7. Why does the Nazarene church practice tithing?
8. What are the duties of the church board?